Have Courage!

Cheri J. Meiners

★

illustrated by Elizabeth Allen

free spirit
PUBLISHING®

Library of Congress Cataloging-in-Publication Data
Meiners, Cheri J., 1957–
    Have courage! / Cheri J. Meiners, M.Ed. ; illustrated by Elizabeth Allen.
       pages cm. — (Being the best me!)
    ISBN-13: 978-1-57542-460-6 (paperback)
    ISBN-10: 1-57542-460-6 (paperback)
    ISBN-13: 978-1-57542-458-3 (hardcover)
    ISBN-10: 1-57542-458-4 (hardcover)
1. Courage in children—Juvenile literature. 2. Courage—Juvenile literature. I. Allen, Elizabeth (Artist) illustrator. II. Title.
    BF723.C694M45 2014
    179'.6—dc23
                                      2014001611

Reading Level Grade 1; Interest Level Ages 4–8;
Fountas & Pinnell Guided Reading Level I

Cover and interior design by Tasha Kenyon
Edited by Marjorie Lisovskis

10 9 8 7 6 5 4 3 2 1
Printed in the United States of America
B10950414

Free Spirit Publishing Inc.
Minneapolis, MN
(612) 338-2068
help4kids@freespirit.com
www.freespirit.com

To my amazing husband and hero, David:
For his courage and passion to do
good in the world.

Even though I'm small,
I can stand tall
and feel good about myself.

I show courage when I do what I think is right—even when it's hard or I feel afraid.

You can sit here.

2

I try to listen to people I trust.

5

If a person dares me to do something
that could hurt someone,
it may take courage *not* to do it.

I can dare to think for myself

and do what I think is best.

I feel brave
when I speak up for myself

and say what I want.

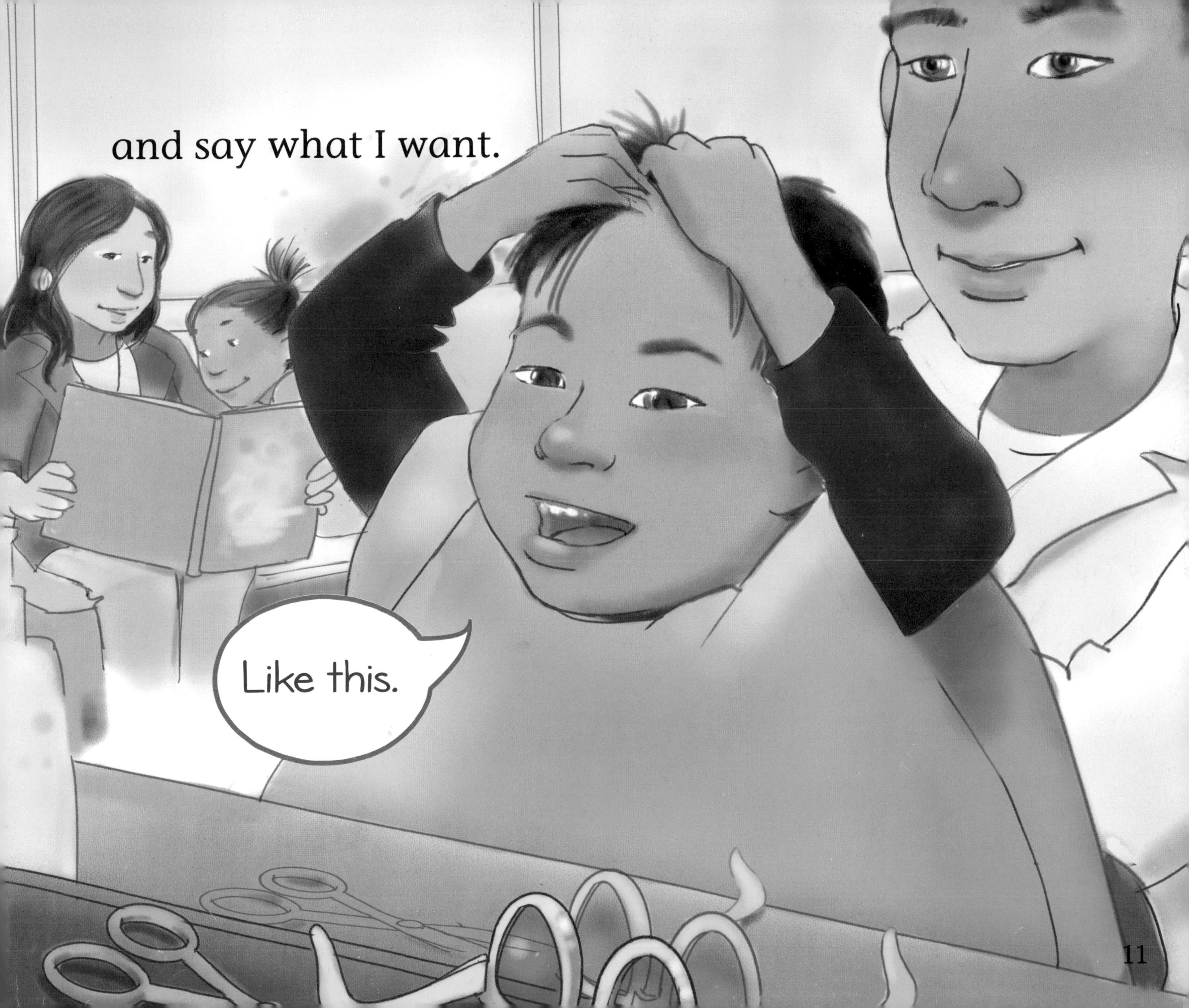

I don't mind if I stand out.

I can dare to just be myself.

I can be brave
and choose to do something hard

because I believe it will be worth it.

When I take a risk
and talk to a child I don't know,

I might make
a friend.

I might even help
someone else feel brave.

When I believe in myself,

I think more about what
I want to do than what
I am afraid of.

If I have the courage
to try something new,
I may start a
fun adventure.

22

I'm glad I know people who can help me.

If something seems safe,

24

I can be brave
and just do it.

FIREWOO

To me, courage is about doing important things that I didn't know I could do.

27

Being brave can help me in everything.

It pushes me
to make good things happen
and be my best.

29

When I have the courage
to do what I believe in,
I can make a difference.

FOOD DRIVE

And I can feel the difference in me.

Ways to Reinforce the Ideas in *Have Courage!*

Have Courage! teaches courage, a resolve that influences the learning and application of all other character traits. Courage can involve physical, intellectual, emotional, or moral challenges. The purpose of the book is to help children understand and feel confident in meeting basic and safe challenges that test their courage and assertiveness.* Specific examples of courage may vary among children depending on what is considered difficult for a given child. However, similar principles and skills can apply to all children. Here is a summary of ten skills discussed in the book that may require courage and that also can help build courage:

1. Stand up for what you think is right.

2. Try something new.

3. Do something even when it is hard.

4. Keep practicing something you are learning.

5. Speak up for your needs.

6. Make the most of a new experience.

7. Dare to make your own decisions.

8. Do something you believe is important.

9. Make a new friend.

10. Help someone else feel brave.

Words to know:

Here are terms you may want to discuss.

bold: daring; not afraid

boldly: strongly and bravely

---

*Adults will, of course, want to be aware and sensitive of real fears that children may face and will want to give comfort and seek help for a child if needed. Additional suggestions for adults to help children deal with fears are provided in *When I Feel Afraid* by Cheri J. Meiners, M.Ed. (Free Spirit Publishing, 2005), pages 32–35.

brave: confident; willing to do something hard

courage: bravery; when you show courage you do something you believe is right, even if it is hard or you feel afraid

courageous: brave; showing or having courage

dare: to push someone to do something that's wrong or risky (page 6); to be brave and do something that's right or necessary (pages 7, 8, and 13)

patient: able to stay calm and not complain when something is hard

persevere: to keep trying and not quit

stand tall: to be brave and proud and strong

As you read each spread, ask children:

• What is happening in this picture?

• What is the main idea?

• How would you feel if you were this person?

Here are additional questions you might discuss:

Pages 1–5

• What does it mean to have courage (to be courageous)?

• What do you think it means to stand tall?

• What is something that's hard for you to do that you try to do anyway?

• What is something that you do when you are asked or when you feel you should—even if you don't really want to?

Pages 6–13

• What does it mean to dare? *(Be sure to discuss both meanings of the word as they are illustrated on page 6 and pages 7 and 8.)*

• Has someone ever said to you, "I dare you to do something?" Did you do it? What happened?

• How could it take more courage *not* to do something that someone dares you to do?

- When is a time that you spoke up about something?

- Why is it important to speak up for yourself when you think something isn't right?

- Why is it important to speak up for yourself when you need something or when something is important to you?

Pages 14–19

- How are you showing courage when you keep doing something and don't give up?

- What is a way you stand out from other people? How does feeling good about yourself help you have courage?

- Why do you think it is helpful to make the most of things that you can't change? How does this show courage?

- Why does it sometimes take courage to make a new friend?

- How can you help someone else feel brave?

Pages 20–31

- What is something new you have tried? How did you like it? Why do people sometimes feel happy after trying something new? How can having courage to try new things make life better?

- How do you feel when you find courage to do something and you just do it? Tell about a time that happened.

- How do you think courage can help in everything we do?

- How can you make a big difference to someone you know?

- How can having courage help you be your best?

- What is something that you want to have more courage to do? What can you do to help yourself find that courage?

Courage Activities and Games

Read this book often with your child or group of children. Once children are familiar with the book, refer to it when opportunities arise for children to show courage. Notice and comment when children show that they understand the meaning of courage and when they speak or act with courage. In addition, use the following activities to reinforce children's understanding of why and how to have courage.

"I Can Be Brave" Pictures

Directions: Discuss situations from the book and everyday fears that children might share. Have children think of something they are afraid of doing. Invite them to tell the others about their fear, if they feel comfortable. (You may want to restate what a child has said to show support or clarify, but do not try to address a child's specific fear at this point. If a child mentions a serious concern, follow up later in a private setting, while redirecting the child to a simpler situation for the group activity.) Talk together and help them think of ways that the fear could be overcome. After discussing several ideas, ask children to draw a picture that shows them overcoming their fear. Pictures could be included in the "Book of Courage" (page 34).

Courage Collage

Materials: Poster paper; magazines; scissors; glue; markers or crayons

Directions: Have or help children cut pictures from magazines that remind them of courage. You may want to prepare by finding several examples they might use. Then make a single group collage or have groups of three or four children make collages. Help children add pictures to the group collage. Invite them to tell you why these pictures remind them of courage. Write or have them write their responses under the pictures.

Finding Heroes

Directions: Ask children to learn a story about a family member, an ancestor, or a friend who displayed courage in a difficult situation. Invite children to report their stories. Ask and discuss questions like "What did the person do to show courage?" and "How can this story help you to have courage?"

Variation: Explore the careers of firefighters, astronauts, police officers, soldiers, athletes, and other occupations that may require courage or bravery. Read and discuss stories of individuals in history who have shown courage and their influence or contribution to society. Let children tell what they admire about each person.

Extension: Discuss with children how men and women in the armed services help keep people safe. They show a great deal of courage and their jobs can be dangerous. Have children write a letter to a serviceman or woman thanking the person for courageous work to protect people. Children may even like to collect small items to send a care package. Several websites give instructions on what to write or send and how to send letters or packages; two of these are operationgratitude.com and anysoldier.com.

Book of Courage

Materials: 8½" by 11" drawing paper; markers or crayons; pencils; 3-hole punch; large 3-ring binder

Directions: After discussing heroes in the "Finding Heroes" activity, have each child draw a picture of someone who shows courage. Possible topics are personal and family stories, general situations such as hazardous occupations, and imaginary situations including superheroes. Children may wish to dictate the courage story, which can be written on the back of the picture.

Compile all the pictures in the binder. You may also want to add pictures from the "'I Can Be Brave' Pictures" activity. Read the book with the children and then add it to your school or home library where they can browse through it regularly.

Variation: Make a large poster or decorate a wall to create a "Wall of Courage" with all the pictures.

My Courage Name

Materials: Index cards; tape

Preparation: Search the Internet for names that mean *courage* or *brave*, or use names from the following list. Write the names on the board. (Do not write the origins or explanations—plan to share those with children during discussion).

Boys
- Abir (Arabic, *courageous*)
- Archibald (German, *bold and daring*)
- Armondo (Spanish, *bold*)
- Bernardo (Portuguese, *brave as a bear*)
- Erol (Turkish, *brave*)
- Jabari (Swahili, *fearless*)
- Leon (French, *lion—symbol of courage*)
- Mato (Native American, *brave*)
- Yong (Chinese, *courage*)

Girls
- Barania (Malaysian, *courage and daring*)
- Drasa (Lithuanian, *courage*)
- Jasura (Arabic, *one of great courage*)
- Kemina (Basque, *strong*)
- Kinga (Hungarian, *bravery*)
- Kumisa (Zulu, *courage*)
- Masha (Yiddish, *brave*)
- Nadine (German, *courage of a bear*)
- Veera (Hindi, *courageous and strong*)

Directions: Tell children that there are names in many languages that mean *courage*. Share the names with the children and explain that they can choose a name to be their special courage name. The name can remind them to have courage whenever they need it. As children select their courage names, write or have them write the name on an index card. The names can be taped to children's desks, tables, or cubbies.

Courage Hat

Materials: Heavy card stock cut into 3" x 20" strips; crayons or markers; stapler; stickers, magazines or old workbooks with pictures, scissors, glue (optional)

Directions: With a crayon or marker, help children write their chosen courage name on the paper strip; then have them color it. If using magazines, have or help children cut and glue pictures or other items that remind them of courage and bravery.

To finish each hat, wrap the strip around the child's head to measure the size. Staple the two ends together to form a ring. Hats can be worn whenever you are discussing courage, as an affirmation when the child has shown courage, or when children need something special to help them feel courageous.

Courage Bracelet

Materials: An assortment of craft letter beads; decorative cording or heavy yarn in various colors; 1 small safety pin or magnetic clasp for each child; heavy tape; scissors

Preparation: For each bracelet, cut three 18-inch strands of cord or yarn that can fit together through your bead; if necessary, use just one or two strands to fit. The finished length of each bracelet will be about 6 to 6½ inches plus excess cord beyond the knots.

Directions: Each bracelet can be made by knotting the three strands together on one end. Tape the knot to a table or firm work surface. Help children braid the strands for about two inches; then add the letter beads. (If using only one or two strands, omit the braiding and just string the beads after tying a knot.) The letter beads can spell the child's name, the special courage name, or even the word *courage*. Continue braiding the strands until the length of the beaded bracelet reaches about 6 inches. Tie a knot in the strands and cut them, leaving about an inch after the knot. Fasten the bracelet to the child's wrist with a safety pin or clasp.

Courage Mascots

Materials: Construction paper in various skin tones; tracing paper; pencils; markers or crayons; scissors; tape

Directions: With your assistance, each child can make a paper doll or action figure that reminds the child to have courage. Have or help children draw a figure and cut it out. If desired, children can use tracing paper to draw and decorate accessories like a hat, boots, a cape, or a coat that will fit over the figure. These can be fastened to the figure with tabs or tape. Children might give the figure their own name or their special courage name. Help children write the name on the back of the figure and write positive statements ("I can have courage," "I can be brave") on the accessories.

Courage Role Plays

Preparation: Prepare scenario cards by writing situations that may require courage on index cards.

Sample Scenarios:

- Blake is nervous about taking swimming lessons.
- Kiki is a little afraid to take the training wheels off her bike.
- Joshua is not sure what it will be like to get a haircut.
- Grace isn't sure what the first day of school will be like.
- It's Juana's first time on the bus and she is a bit scared.
- Henry feels shy about talking to a child on the playground.
- Yuan is nervous about going up to a worker in a store and asking a question.
- Gabriella is a little scared about going to the dentist.

Level 1

Select or have a child select a scenario card and use it to describe a scene for children. For example: "Blake is taking swimming lessons but he is afraid and won't get in the water" or "It's Juana's first time on the bus and she is a little scared, so she takes a deep breath and climbs up the steps." Ask, "Did this person show courage? Why or why not?"

Level 2

Help a child select and read a scenario card. Ask questions like these: "What could this person do?" "How does that show courage?" "Who might the child ask to help?" Prompt courageous responses if needed. If you wish, let children use dolls and action figures to act out the scenario.

Level 3

After completing a scenario in Level 2, say to children, "Imagine this happened to you. How could *you* respond with courage in this situation?" Help children act out the scenario.

Free Spirit's Being the Best Me! Series

Books that help young children develop character traits and attitudes that strengthen self-confidence, resilience, decision-making, and a sense of purpose. *Each book: 40 pp., color illust., HC and PB, 11¼" x 9¼", ages 4–8.*

Be Positive!
Guide young children to develop a positive outlook

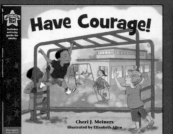

Feel Confident!
Empower children to recognize their individual worth and develop confidence

Cheri J. Meiners • illustrated by Elizabeth Allen

Have Courage!
Help children develop the attitudes and skills of assertiveness

Cheri J. Meiners
illustrated by Elizabeth Allen

Bounce Back!
Foster perseverance, patience, and resilience with this unique, encouraging book

Cheri J. Meiners • illustrated by Elizabeth Allen

Free Spirit's Learning to Get Along® Series by Cheri J. Meiners

Help children learn, understand, and practice basic social and emotional skills. Real-life situations, diversity, and concrete examples make these read-aloud books appropriate for childcare settings, schools, and the home. *Each book: 40 pp., color illust., PB, 9" x 9", ages 4–8.*

Accept and Value Each Person
Introduces diversity and related concepts: respecting differences, being inclusive, and appreciating people just the way they are.

Be Careful and Stay Safe
Teaches children how to avoid potential dangers, ask for help, follow directions, use things carefully, and plan ahead.

Be Honest and Tell the Truth
Children learn that being honest in words and actions builds self-confidence and trust, and that telling the truth can take courage and tact.

Be Polite and Kind
Introduces children to good manners and gracious behavior including saying "Please," "Thank you," "Excuse me," and "I'm sorry."

Cool Down and Work Through Anger
Teaches skills for working through anger: self-calming, getting help, talking and listening, apologizing, and viewing others positively.

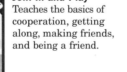

Join In and Play
Teaches the basics of cooperation, getting along, making friends, and being a friend.

Know and Follow Rules
Shows children that following rules can help us stay safe, learn, be fair, get along, and instill a positive sense of pride.

Listen and Learn
Introduces and explains what listening means, why it's important to listen, and how to listen well.

Reach Out and Give
Begins with the concept of gratitude; shows children contributing to their community in simple yet meaningful ways.

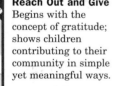

Respect and Take Care of Things
Children learn to put things where they belong and ask permission to use things. Teaches simple environmental awareness.

Share and Take Turns
Gives reasons to share; describes four ways to share; points out that children can also share their knowledge, creativity, and time.

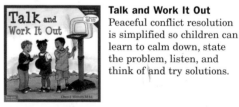

Talk and Work It Out
Peaceful conflict resolution is simplified so children can learn to calm down, state the problem, listen, and think of and try solutions.

Try and Stick with It
Introduces children to flexibility, stick-to-it-iveness (perseverance), and the benefits of trying something new.

Understand and Care
Builds empathy in children; guides them to show they care by listening to others and respecting their feelings.

When I Feel Afraid
Helps children understand their fears; teaches simple coping skills; encourages children to talk with trusted adults about their fears.

Learning to Get Along® Series Interactive Software
Children follow along or read on their own, using a special highlight feature to click or hear word definitions. User's Guide included. *For Mac and Windows.*

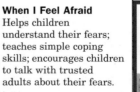

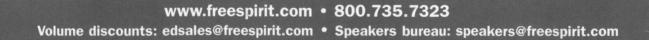

www.freespirit.com • 800.735.7323
Volume discounts: edsales@freespirit.com • Speakers bureau: speakers@freespirit.com

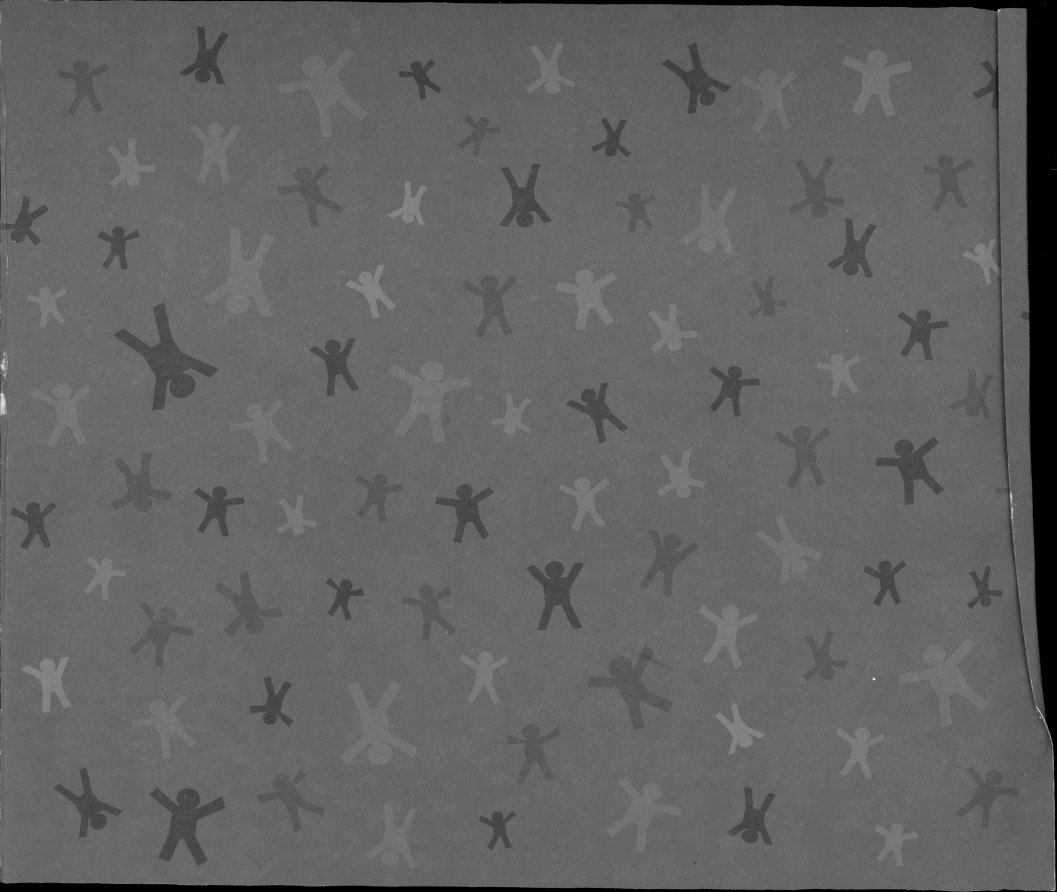